D1154419

My Life Cycle

My Life as a
SEA TURTLE

PICTURE WINDOW BOOKS

a capstone imprint

Published by Picture Window Books, an imprint of Capstone.
1710 Roe Crest Drive, North Mankato, Minnesota 56003
capstonepub.com

Copyright © 2023 by Capstone. All rights reserved. No part of this publication may be reproduced in whole or in part, or stored in a retrieval system, or transmitted in any form or by any means, electronic, mechanical, photocopying, recording, or otherwise, without written permission of the publisher.

Library of Congress Cataloging-in-Publication Data
Names: Sazaklis, John, author. | Pang, Bonnie, illustrator.
Title: My life as a sea turtle / by John Sazaklis ; illustrated by Bonnie Pang.
Description: North Mankato, Minnesota : Picture Window Books, [2023] | Series: My life cycle | Includes index. | Audience: Ages 5–7 | Audience: Grades K–1 | Summary: "Hi, there! I'm a sea turtle. I spend most of my days surfing in warm waters, but I started life much smaller! Learn more about my life cycle and how I went from a tiny little egg to a hatchling to an adult."— Provided by publisher.
Identifiers: LCCN 2022000809 (print) | LCCN 2022000810 (ebook) | ISBN 9781666340419 (hardcover) | ISBN 9781666340495 (pdf) | ISBN 9781666340518 (kindle edition)
Subjects: LCSH: Sea turtles—Life cycles—Juvenile literature.
Classification: LCC QL666.C536 S354 2023 (print) | LCC QL666.C536 (ebook) | DDC 597.92/8156—dc23/eng/20220207
LC record available at https://lccn.loc.gov/2022000809
LC ebook record available at https://lccn.loc.gov/2022000810

Editorial Credits
Editor: Alison Deering; Designer: Kay Fraser; Media Researcher: Svetlana Zhurkin; Production Specialist: Katy LaVigne

Printed and bound in the USA. 4882

My Life as a
SEA TURTLE

by John Sazaklis

illustrated by Bonnie Pang

Hi there! I am a green sea turtle. Other sea turtles like me have been around for 100 million years. We knew the dinosaurs!

I have a BIG extended family. Let me introduce you to some of my relatives . . .

First up are leatherback sea turtles. They are the largest. They can grow up to 7 feet (2 meters) long. They can weigh 2,000 pounds (900 kilograms)!

leatherback
turtle

flatback turtle

Flatback sea turtles have flat shells.

Hawksbill sea turtles have curved, pointed beaks.

hawksbill turtle

loggerhead turtle

Loggerheads have large heads and strong jaws.

I get *my* name thanks to my diet. I love eating greens! They give my skin an emerald color.

Green sea turtles are some of the largest in the world.
But I wasn't always this big . . .

My mom lays her eggs on a warm summer night. She uses her clawed flippers to bury us in the sand. There are about 100 of us squished in there.

Burying us protects us from **predators**. Crabs, raccoons, and seagulls might gobble us up!

Then, Mom swims back into the sea. We're on our own now. Bye, bye babies!

Inside the egg, I begin to grow. I eat the leftover yolk for strength. It takes me about two months to hatch.

Finally, **CRACK!** I break out of my shell.

I am a **hatchling**. I measure about 2 inches (5 centimeters) long. I weigh only 8 ounces (227 grams). I could fit in the palm of your hand!

My siblings and I wait until nighttime to head to the water. The brightest line of the **horizon** points us in the right direction.

It takes another six to eight weeks to reach the open ocean. Talk about slow motion!

All that swimming makes me hungry. I eat **plankton**, **mollusks**, jellyfish, and fish eggs. *MMM!*

At 3 to 9 months old, I am a toddler turtle. I weigh just over 10.5 ounces (300 g). I measure about 5 inches (13 cm) long.

Atlantic Ocean

I surf toward the Sargasso Sea in the Atlantic Ocean. There, I blend into the green seaweed. It's a feast of seaweed, shrimp, and fish!

The sun heats the water's surface. I need the warm water to live and grow.

At age 5, I am a **juvenile**. I measure 8 to 12 inches (20 to 30 cm) long. That's about the size of a dinner plate!

I have a hard top shell to protect me. It is green, olive, and brown. My bottom shell is yellowish white.

I also have flippers. They help me swim as fast as 22 miles (35 kilometers) per hour. They can even hold my food. I use my hind feet to guide as I glide.

Green sea turtles mostly stay in water. I can spend up to five hours underwater before I need to come up for air. I can also drink salt water. I filter the salt through **glands** behind my eyes.

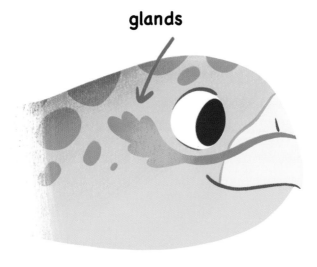

glands

Alaska

You can find turtles in the Pacific Ocean from California to Alaska. We also hang out in the Atlantic Ocean from Texas to Massachusetts.

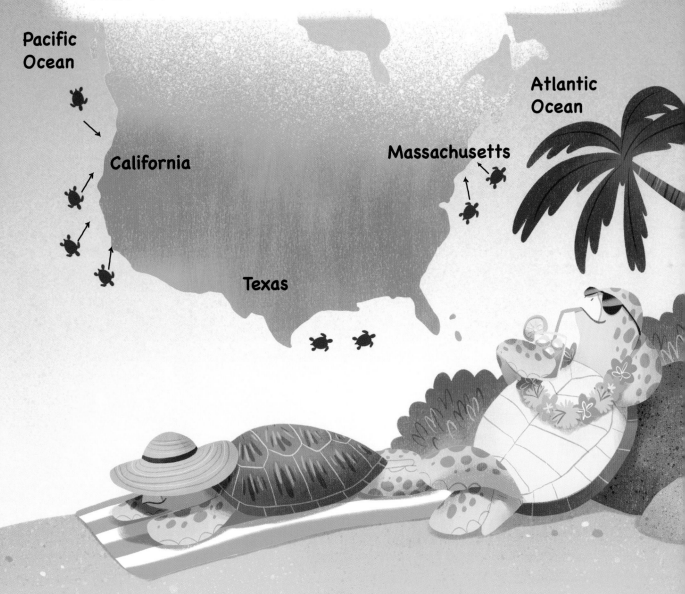

Pacific Ocean

Atlantic Ocean

California

Massachusetts

Texas

My cousins in Hawaii are a little different. They like to climb on the beach and sunbathe!

I become an adult at 25 years old. I can be 3 to 4 feet (1 to 1.2 m) long. I can weigh up to 350 pounds (159 kg). I am a complete **herbivore**. I eat algae, seagrass, and sponges.

Eventually, it's time for me to find a mate. This usually happens in late spring or early summer. I use Earth's magnetic forces to find my way back to where I was born. That's like a sea turtle superpower!

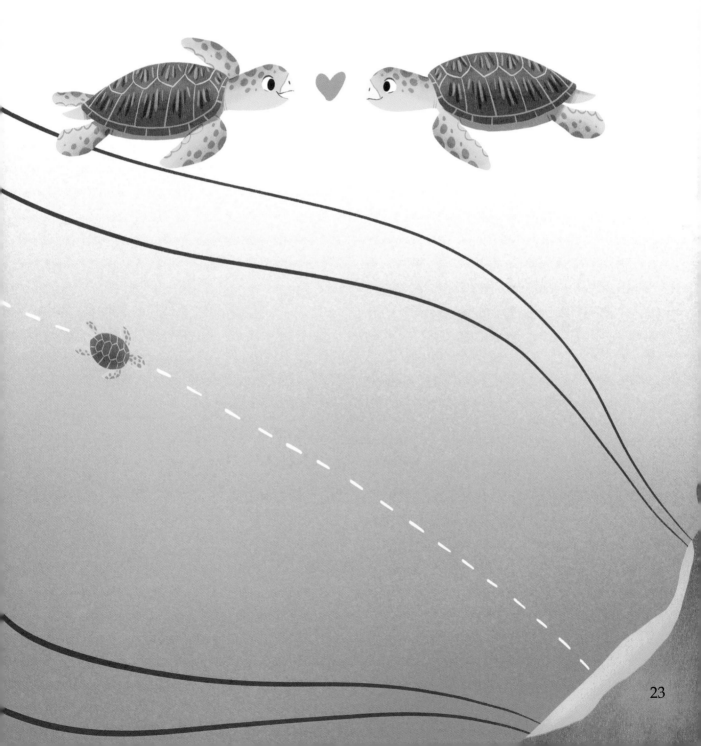

After my mate and I meet, I do what my mom did. I crawl out to the sand at night and dig a hole for my own batch of eggs.

Our nesting areas are found in warm waters around the globe—from the Caribbean to the Great Barrier Reef in Australia.

Caribbean

Australia

I can live for 70 years—or more! But it can be tough out there for a turtle. Did you know that I am an **endangered** species?

You can help keep me safe by protecting the beaches where I nest. Make your turtle team and go green!

My Life as a Sea Turtle

About the Author

John Sazaklis is a *New York Times* bestselling author with more than 100 children's books under his utility belt! He has also illustrated Spider-Man books, created toys for *MAD* magazine, and written for the BEN 10 animated series. John lives in New York City with his superpowered wife and daughter, who recently joined forces with him to voice the Grinch and Whos in the interactive board book *Dr. Seuss's The Sounds of Grinchmas: With 12 Silly Sounds!*

About the Illustrator

Bonnie Pang is an illustrator and comic artist from Hong Kong. She currently illustrates children's books and creates the webcomic *IT Guy & ART Girl*. When not drawing, she enjoys watching movies, gardening, and exploring new places.

Glossary

endangered (in-DAYN-juhrd)—in danger of dying out

gland (GLAND)—an organ in the body that makes certain chemicals

hatchling (HACH-ling)—a young animal that has just come out of its egg

herbivore (HUR-buh-vor)—an animal that eats only plants

horizon (huh-RYE-zuhn)—the line where the sky and the earth or sea seem to meet

juvenile (JOO-vuh-nuhl)—a young animal

mollusk (MOL-uhsk)—a soft-bodied creature that usually has a shell

plankton (PLANGK-tuhn)—tiny plants and animals that drift in the sea

predator (PRED-uh-tur)—an animal that hunts other animals for food

index